Bill Putnam is Principal Lecturer in Archaeology at Dorset Institute of Higher Education and is Chairman of the Trust for Wessex Archaeology. He is well known for his lectures on Dorset's archaeology and directed the eleven-year excavation of the Dewlish Roman villa near Puddletown.

Frontispiece: *Lysons 1796 drawing of one of the mosaic floors of Frampton Roman villa.*

ROMAN DORSET

BILL PUTNAM

DOVECOTE PRESS

First published in 1984 by The Dovecote Press Ltd
Stanbridge, Wimborne, Dorset
ISBN 0 946159 27 0

© Bill Putnam 1984

Designed by Humphrey Stone
Photoset by Megaron Typesetting, Bournemouth
Printed and bound in Great Britain by Biddles Ltd,
Guildford and King's Lynn

CONTENTS

ACKNOWLEDGEMENTS

Acknowledgements and thanks are due to: Maureen Putnam, for help with the preparation of the book; Dorset County Museum, for providing the bulk of the illustrations and helping in many other ways, including permitting the use of Peter Woodward's reconstruction drawings of Dewlish villa and the industrial site on Purbeck; the estate of the late Alan Sorrell for the reconstruction drawings of Maiden Castle and road making; Ted Flatters for the photograph of the mosaic from Olga Road, Dorchester; Dorset Institute of Higher Education for the Dewlish villa photographs; Poole Museums for the photograph of excavations at Lake Farm, Wimborne; Cambridge University, Department of Aerial Photographs for the photographs of Badbury Rings and Bokerley Dyke, W.J. White for the photographs of the Hinton St Mary mosaic.

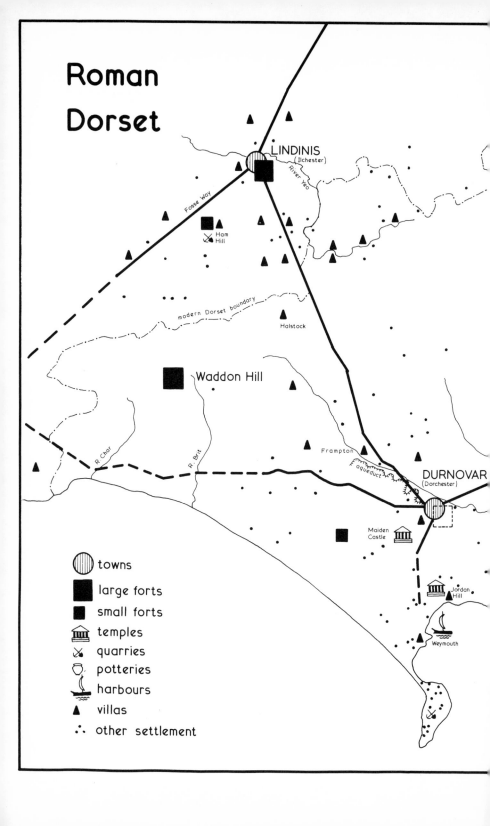

Roman
Dorset

LINDINIS
(Ilchester)

River Yeo

Fosse Way

Ham
Hill

modern Dorset boundary

Halstock

Waddon Hill

R. Char

R. Brit

Frampton

aqueduct

DURNOVAR
(Dorchester)

Maiden
Castle

Jordan
Hill

Weymouth

towns
large forts
small forts
temples
quarries
potteries
harbours
villas
other settlement

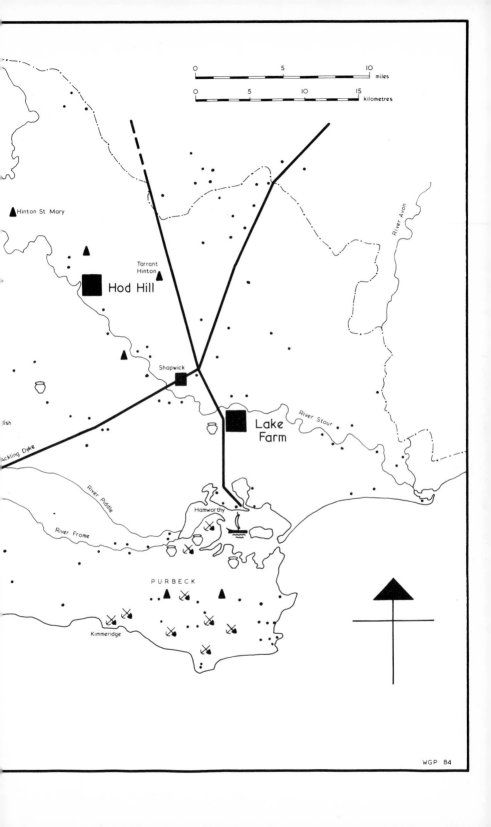

miles

kilometres

Hinton St Mary

Tarrant
Hinton

Hod Hill

Shapwick

River Avon

River Stour

Lake
Farm

Ackling Dyke

lish

River Piddle

River Frome

Hamworthy

P U R B E C K

Kimmeridge

WGP 84

I

THE DUROTRIGES

Throughout this book the word 'Dorset' will be used as it is short and simple; but the reader should remember that the territory of the Iron Age tribe of the Durotriges was a little larger than modern Dorset. It extended to the Avon in the east, the Wylye in the north, and at least as far as the Axe in the west. The hillforts of Ham Hill and South Cadbury, both in Somerset, were certainly Durotrigian.

Human settlement has existed in Dorset since at least 4,000 BC. The inhabitants of the Neolithic (New Stone Age) and Bronze Ages built the burial mounds which are still a prominent feature of the landscape. However, we know all too little about where they actually lived.

The place we now call Dorchester was chosen by the Romans for their capital, and a city was built there for the first time; but its significance as a tribal centre may in fact go back a lot further, to Neolithic times. Maumbury Rings, later to become a Roman amphitheatre, began life as a Neolithic henge monument, similar to the earliest stage of Stonehenge. Mount Pleasant, on the eastern outskirts of the town, was the site of another major henge, and in the 1984 excavations by the Trust for Wessex Archaeology in Greyhound Yard, Dorchester, a huge Neolithic building was found, built of tree trunks let three metres into the ground.

Nevertheless, it is on the whole unlikely that the identity of the Durotriges can be traced as far back as that.

It may seem surprising that we can put a name to a prehistoric tribe at all! But though their early days were before history, once they came into contact with the Greek and Roman world — and this happened through trade long before the invasion of 43 AD — then written records of their name became possible.

Even so, we are lucky to know their name at all; it only occurs in three places; on two building inscriptions put up by Durotrigian work parties on Hadrian's Wall, and in the *Geography* of Ptolemy, a Greek writing in Alexandria about 150 AD. Ptolemy and one of the wall stones calls them Durotriges; the second wall stone (from Housesteads) calls them Durotrages. Durotrages must remain a possibility, but they are usually known as the Durotriges.

Since we know so little of them, how can we define their territory? There are two main ways of doing this; first by the location of finds of their characteristic dark brown or black burnished pottery, and secondly by finds of their own distinctive coins. These were silver staters and quarter-staters, but unlike the tribes in south-eastern Britain, they had not taken to inscribing their kings' names or names of their cities in Latin letters. As far as we know, they were illiterate.

In the last centuries before the Roman conquest they were certainly engaged in trade with the continent, particularly the Armorican peninsula (Brittany). Coins of Armorican tribes are occasionally found in Dorset, and large quantities of continental pottery were imported through the trading centre in the promontory fort at Hengistbury Head.

The Durotriges almost certainly helped Armorica in their revolt against the Romans in 56 BC,.and in this fact may lie a clue to their origins.

It used to be fashionable to imagine that every new group of people identified in Britain came here by way of violent invasion; but it is now realised that this is not necessarily the case.

In origin the Durotriges were probably a mixture of the indigenous people of Dorset (themselves already a mixture) with new groups, arriving from Armorica. They came initially to trade, later to settle and intermarry with the locals. A similar process has gone on ever since!

The knowledge of iron had arrived in Dorset as early as 700 BC and this too may reflect the arrival of a group of people who became part of the Durotriges who awaited the Roman invasion in 43 AD.

Thus we have Durotrigian Dorset, a distinct tribal area, fiercely defended, with its own coinage entirely different to the coinage of the Belgic tribes to the east. The Durotriges had a successful pottery industry that was to rise to even greater heights under Roman control. Their kings and lesser chieftains lived in heavily defended hillforts, which had gone some way to becoming towns.

Their population was large and they were prospering. It must not be thought that they all lived in the hillforts; the whole countryside was a network of farms and villages, and the small rectangular fields of their farms covered much of the landscape, including many areas which we tend to think of as being cultivated for the first time since the Second World War.

But all said and done, they were still an Iron Age tribe, living in what most people today would find quite intolerable conditions, close to nature and often in fear of attack. This is illustrated by one of the commonest features of Iron Age sites, the grain storage pit. Here the harvest was stored; the tops were camouflaged, in the hope of saving their food in time of danger.

In the early summer of 43 AD (not that they named the years in that way!) horsemen galloped from farm to farm, warning of an impending invasion that was to take more from them than their food supplies. The value of what it brought to them is a matter of debate.

II

THE ROMAN CONQUEST

In 43 AD the Durotriges suffered one of the most frightening experiences ever to befall the county.

The Romans had for many years ruled over the tribes in Gaul and to some extent in Germany. In fact the Gauls were themselves half-Roman by now, the great days of Vercingetorix's revolt against Caesar already beyond living memory.

But the Channel, part of the Roman 'Ocean' which surrounded their known world, lay between the Romans and the island of Britannia. Caesar, after enormous difficulty with the tides in the Channel (unfamiliar to Mediterranean sailors) had raided Britain in 55 BC, and returned in 54 to conquer the south-eastern part, including the capital at Wheathampstead of its king Cassivellaunus.

But political and military pressures on the continent took him back to Rome and the British conquest did not survive in contrast to Gaul, which became part of the Roman Empire.

For 97 years the tribes of Britain remained independent, though with increasing trade connections with the Roman world.

Then in 43 AD another Roman ruler, the emperor Claudius, found it expedient to return to Britain and complete Caesar's conquest.

Many have wondered why he did it. Archaeological evidence can rarely supply the answer to such a question, but fortunately written history survives of the period, especially the Histories of Dio Cassius.

Claudius needed a military victory to gain the support of the soldiers on whom his power depended, and probably this was the main reason behind the invasion. A pretext occurred in the form of an appeal for Roman help from a British prince, and the invasion began in early July.

THE INVASION

Claudius did not command in person, but appointed his best general, Aulus Plautius, to command the army and become the first governor of the new province.

Four legions crossed the Channel. These were II Augusta, IX Hispana, XIV Gemina and XX Valeria Victrix. All were drawn from other provinces where they were not needed. A legion was between 5,000 and 6,000 strong, and since they would have been accompanied by a similar number of auxiliary troops (archers, slingers, light infantry and cavalry) the total size of the force was about 45,000 men.

The Roman intelligence services had learnt much from Caesar's experience and trading contacts since that time. Few mistakes were made and by early September Claudius had arrived in person to take charge in response to a pre-planned "appeal" for help from Aulus Plautius; Claudius routed the enemy (led by Cogodumnus and Caractacus, the sons of Cunobelinus, Shakespeare's Cymbeline) and entered Colchester in triumph. Colchester (Camulodunum) had by then become the capital of the Catuvellauni, the dominant tribe of southern Britain.

This Belgic group of tribes, themselves a threat to the Durotriges, had all been defeated or had submitted to suit their own ends. We do not know the exact movements of the four legions, but late in the year a legion which was almost certainly II Augusta was pouring its supplies ashore at Hamworthy and setting up bases on the fringe of the already conquered territory of the Atrebates to the east.

The Durotriges not surprisingly resisted grimly. They had had little contact with Rome and had not been involved in the political manoeuvrings of recent years. The Roman invaders represented a threat as fearsome as that presented to the British by the German armies in 1940.

The Romans planned, at least initially, a province formed from the more developed Belgic tribes of the south-east, but for military reasons the frontier was drawn along a line from Lincoln to Seaton in Devon, and we now know that frontier as the Fosse Way.

Unfortunately for the Durotriges, their territory was within the frontier; in any case their heavily fortified hilltop towns could not be left untouched on the Romans' southern flank.

THE WAR AGAINST THE DUROTRIGES

The result was a bitter war of conquest fought over a period as long as 15 years and culminating in a last rebellion at the time of Boudica's campaign of 60 AD, which left its bloody remains in the gateway of the hillfort at South Cadbury in Somerset.

The main base of Legio II Augusta seems to have been at Lake Farm, on the banks of the Stour at Wimborne. Here excavations by

Poole Museums along the line of the Wimborne bypass have shown a tantalising glimpse of the defences and the barrack blocks of a large fortress. Geophysical surveys of the meadows by the river suggest that the fortress covered 12 hectares (about 29 acres). This is big enough for a full legion when camping briefly on the march, but with wooden barrack blocks as were seen in the excavation, half a legion is a more likely size for the force stationed there.

Lake Farm was very likely the main base for the Durotrigian campaign, with a vexillation of the legion (perhaps five of its ten cohorts) held there in reserve, together with legionary headquarters. The remaining cohorts were distributed in smaller forts in advance of Lake Farm.

The Lake Farm fortress is connected by a well authenticated Roman road (see chapter 5) directly to the sea at Hamworthy, where some military stores have been found at the harbour site.

We can name the commander *(legatus legionis)* of legio II Augusta at the time of the invasion, something rarely possible in the

Modern excavation by Poole Museums; the narrow trenches are the foundations of the timber barrack blocks of the second legion at Lake Farm, near Wimborne.

The emperor Vespasian, seen here on a coin. As commander of the second Augustan legion he was responsible for the invasion of Dorset.

story of Roman Britain. He was Vespasian, later to become emperor, and a very good one at that. His life is described in eulogistic terms by the writer Suetonius, who says 'he went to Britain, where he fought thirty battles, conquered two warlike tribes, and captured more than twenty towns, besides the whole of the Isle of Wight'.

This suggests Vespasian completed the conquest of the Durotriges in his brief stay, but the archaeological evidence shows it took much longer. The Durotriges are not mentioned of course, but the Isle of Wight confirms that he came in this direction and the twenty *oppida* he captured must surely have been the great hillforts of the Durotriges.

Several of these hillforts have revealed traces of the violent assaults that occurred. Undoubtedly the most spectacular evidence is provided by Hod Hill near Blandford. Here excavations by the British Museum in the 1950's showed that one of the cohorts of Legio II accompanied by a regiment of cavalry was stationed here in an unusual fort built actually inside the ramparts of the hillfort. From the air the contour-hugging native ramparts and the neat and efficient Roman defences provide a sharp contrast. It is visually the most dramatic site in the whole of the conquest story. No one knows why the Roman commander used the native defences for two sides of his enclosure.

Clearly the Durotrigian inhabitants were no longer there when the Roman fort was built. They were dead, or scattered in the countryside waging guerilla warfare. The excavations found many iron heads of *ballista* bolts, the heavy mechanically fired arrows of the legion's light artillery. Significantly a large group were concentrated in one particular native hut which had its own enclosure within the hillfort; it may well be that the barrage was concentrated on the chieftain's hut.

The Roman occupation of Hod Hill lasted less than ten years, during which it was at first part of the defensive screen round Lake Farm, and later part of the controlling network of forts in Durotrigian territory. This latter task was taken over by Waddon Hill near Beaminster in the early fifties, and the same units may have been moved to Waddon.

Some of the buildings at Hod Hill were burnt down, and much equipment left lying about the fort. Perhaps it ended in disaster from a Durotrigian attack, but it is all too easy to assume that burnt buildings mean an enemy attack. They may have been burnt by accident or burnt to clear the site.

A similar fort existed at Waddon Hill, and was occupied from the early fifties till about 60 AD, the year of the great Boudican rebellion. Excavations here were carried out by Dr Graham Webster in the 1960's, and found a similar type of fort to Hod Hill, though this time on a new site.

Hod Hill, near Blandford. The main outline is that of the Iron Age hillfort, and in the bottom part the streets and huts can be distinguished. In the top right hand corner lies the very different fortifications of the Roman fort inserted into it. This housed a cohort of the second legion and a regiment of cavalry.

Both Hod Hill and Waddon Hill are unusual; Roman forts in Britain are to be found on lower ground, within easy reach of road transport particularly at road junctions and river crossings. Hod Hill and Waddon Hill lie on hilltops, difficult of access and unconnected to the known Roman road system. This must reflect the tactical problems of the Durotrigian campaign; at times the situation may well have been one of extreme difficulty.

Other such forts must have existed. Probably one has been quarried away at Ham Hill, near Ilminster. Roman military buildings existed at South Cadbury, but it is not clear how extensive they were. Yet others may exist undetected or destroyed, and some smaller forts are known.

DORCHESTER

Dorchester did not exist at this time. It is certain that the Roman army built a base somewhere near the site of the later town, but exactly what and where provides one of the most tantalising puzzles of the whole story.

The evidence is as follows:

1. Finds in Dorchester of the period of the emperor Claudius, including a splendid bone sword handle.
2. Finds of Claudian date in Weymouth.
3. The undoubted Roman road connecting Weymouth to Dorchester which is reminiscent of the similar seaborne supply arrangement at Hamworthy.
4. The fact that over 90% of the towns of Roman Britain occupy sites used at first for forts.
5. The fact that the Roman road from London to the later fortress of the Second Legion at Exeter passes through Dorchester.
6. The find at Whitcombe, near Dorchester, of a carved stone which looks very like part of a cavalryman's tombstone (though it may be too late in date).
7. The existence in the structure of the church at Godmanstone of a re-used altar stone dedicated to *Jupiter Optimus Maximus* by a centurion (though it refers to a legion other than II Augusta).
8. Maumbury Rings at Dorchester which, though it started life as a Neolithic henge monument, was altered by the Romans into an amphitheatre.

The excavations at Maumbury Rings at the turn of the century have recently been reassessed and properly published. Though one might expect the amphitheatre to have been built at the time of the development of the civilian town in the seventies (see Chapter 4) the archaeological evidence seems to point to an earlier date in the fifties or sixties.

If this is so — and it is not by any means certain — then only one body could have built such a structure, and that is Legio II Augusta. What is more it seats about 6,000, and would imply that either the whole or at least the second half of the legion was based long enough at or near Dorchester for such buildings to be constructed.

The Legion would have called it the *ludus*. Although no doubt let out for entertainment purposes, its primary function would have been for military training, demonstrations, drill, and displays. Was the Legion in Dorchester? The problem is that nowhere in or around the town have the defences or barrack blocks of such a substantial fortress been found, in spite of the extensive excavations in various quarters of the town in recent years.

One of the exciting things about archaeology is that at any moment a new discovery may throw into confusion one's most cherished ideas, and perhaps by the time these words appear in print some new discovery will have been made, which clears up the mystery of the Roman fort at Dorchester, or perhaps puts the problem in a new light.

Buckle from a Roman soldier's belt; evidence of the presence of the army in Dorchester.

It may have been from the new base on the Frome (wherever it was) that the Romans launched their attack on Maiden Castle, certainly the most famous of the Durotrigian hillforts.

Sir Mortimer Wheeler's excavations here in the 1930's provided grim details about the Roman assault. The Durotrigians attempted in vain to defend their hillfort against an army which was trained and equipped to storm much more sophisticated defences than those of Maiden Castle.

It is likely that only one cohort of the legion would have been needed; certainly part of the legion was present, as several defenders were killed by the ballista bolts of its artillery. No elaborate siege works were needed, or the traces would survive today; probably the legionaries formed a *testudo* ('tortoise' formation with shields locked over their heads) and approached the gates. They may have sawn through the bolts, or lit a fire to burn them, or battered them down with a ram. All the time volleys of ballista bolts swept the ramparts, killing those who rashly stood in view.

It was one of these men whose body was found by Wheeler, the spine still dramatically pierced by the head of the bolt which killed

The Iron Age hillfort of Maiden Castle seen from the south. The east gate where the assault took place is to the right, and the foundations of the Roman temple can just be seen on the far side.

The Roman attack on Maiden Castle as imagined by the artist Alan Sorrell.

The cemetery in the eastern entrance to Maiden Castle, as uncovered by Sir Mortimer Wheeler in the 1930's. The defenders were buried by their own people with food for their journey to another world.

Close up of one of the skeletons from the Maiden Castle cemetery. Piercing one of the vertebrae is the iron head of a bolt fired from a legionary ballista, the most dramatic evidence imaginable of the Roman attack.

him. He lay with 37 others, men and women, buried in the eastern entrance to the hillfort. But clearly the defenders had surrendered in time for some at least to survive, because the dead were buried in the Durotrigian tradition with pots full of food to accompany them on their journey to another world.

THE END OF THE CAMPAIGN

It is a mistake to imagine the Roman army patrolling Dorset throughout the three and a half centuries that Britain was part of the Roman empire.

There is no evidence of any of the forts being occupied after about 65 AD, and even the legionary fortress at Exeter is abandoned soon after that, and Legio II Augusta moved, first to Gloucester, and finally (in 75 AD) to its permanent home in Caerleon in South Wales.

By the mid-seventies the civilian towns were being built, and Romanization was in full swing. Clearly by then the battle was won by the Romans, and Dorset was becoming fully integrated into the Roman world. The soldiers moved away to the north, where they remained permanently on guard.

But at least in the north of the territory of the Durotriges there is evidence at South Cadbury of a last stand, which left its dead lying unburied in the south-west gateway. This may have been in 60 AD, when Boudica, Queen of the Iceni of Norfolk, led her people and many others in a final attempt to gain their freedom. All available Roman troops were dispatched to the midlands, where under the command of Suetonius Paulinus they ultimately defeated Boudica.

We are told that the legion from the south-west did not arrive, and its commander committed suicide. Perhaps his soldiers were pinned down as they faced the last desperate rebellion by the Durotriges of Dorset and were unable to march north.

III
ROMAN GOVERNMENT

THE CIVITAS

The Romans chose as their units of 'self-government' in Britain the native tribes as they existed before the invasion. Some had welcomed the Romans, and were rewarded with a special 'client King' status for their leaders. Among these were Cogidubnus in Sussex and Prasutagus in Norfolk. Others, which resisted strongly, were more harshly treated. But the privileged tribes lost their privileges when their original leader died, and all ended as normal *civitates* in the Roman province.

Each civitas had its capital, and in the case of the Durotriges (as we shall see in chapter 4) this was Durnovaria, or Dorchester. We cannot define the tribal territory exactly, but it included present Dorset plus a little bit of Somerset, Wiltshire, Hampshire and Devon. Essentially its identity has remained with us till today. Our knowledge of its extent depends on the distribution pattern of the native coins and the distinct style of pottery.

The civitas capitals were the lowest grade of town in the province. Above them came the *Municipia*, towns rewarded by the grant of Latin Citizenship, an inferior form of Roman Citizenship. Verulamium is the only known example. Above them were the *Coloniae*, cities actually formed from Roman citizens. The first of these was Colchester, no doubt populated by veterans of Claudius' invading army. Later came Lincoln, Gloucester and York.

CITIZENSHIP

The citizens of Durnovaria had to be content with citizenship of their own tribe, the Durotriges. Full Roman citizenship was something very much coveted, in view of the privileges it brought. Everyone knows the story of St Paul, taken to Rome to a hearing before the emperor because of his citizenship. The only tombstone from Durnovaria records Carinus, a Roman citizen. The size of the letters indicates the importance of his citizenship.

There was one principal way of gaining Roman citizenship and that was by service in the army. The auxiliary regiments were formed from non-citizens, and after 25 years service the reward was citizenship for the soldier and for his wife and children. No doubt Durotrigians would have been among the British regiments found serving in various parts of the empire.

However soon after 200 AD the emperor Caracalla granted citizenship to all those within the empire, and this distinction became less important.

Not only were the inhabitants of Dorset citizens of their own civitas, but they were governed under native or Celtic law, not under Roman law. Celtic law was that of the native tribe as modified by the Roman government to match their own system. And on a capital charge a citizen had the right of appeal to the governor, in the same way as the Roman citizen could appeal to the emperor.

Everyday justice among the Durotriges was then more or less according to traditional Celtic law, and administered by Durotrigian judges. The governor went on circuit during the winter, when the armies were not campaigning, and no doubt from time to time the governor sat in judgement in Durnovaria. After the time of Agricola (77-84 AD) the appeal cases may well have been heard by the *legatus iuridicus*, a lawyer appointed to help the governor with his legal duties.

THE COUNCIL

The Durotriges were governed by a 'county' council, similar in functions to the modern one, but rather less democratic in its workings! This was called the *Ordo* or the order. Its name and the names of its officers were similar to those of cities all over the Roman world.

Its members, theoretically 100, but usually fewer, were *decurions*. These were the elders and nobles of the Durotrigian tribe, retaining their position of privilege. Membership depended on a property qualification. They became, at least on the surface, more fully Romanized than the rest of the people. They owned the rich town houses with elaborate mosaic floors; many also owned a rich country house, or *villa*. Much of the trade and its profits were in their hands, as it had been before the conquest. We cannot, alas, put a name to a single one of them. The nearest we can really get to them is to admire the mosaics which graced their living room floors. For them the conquest meant a dramatic change in lifestyle, unlike the poorer people in the countryside.

The *ordo* made policy of its own accord in limited local areas of

27

government, but more often interpreted centrally issued edicts of the governor or emperor. Perhaps in the last years of Roman Britain, as central government broke down, they came into their own, but we know little of it.

THE MAGISTRATES

Their chief executives were known as *Duoviri Iuridicundo*. *Duo* means two, and in accordance with Roman tradition of public office there were two of them, as of every other office. Either could veto the actions of the other. A curious system to our way of thinking, but designed to prevent abuse of office. For a similar reason the posts were annual. The duovirs administered local justice and presided at meetings of the ordo and the public assembly *(comitia)*. They were responsible for public shows and the great religious festivals.

In addition there were two *aediles* or public works officers, who ran the roads, the drains, and the water supply, and looked after public buildings. Two *quaestors* may have looked after local finances, but most taxation was collected by contractors on behalf of central government. Every fifth year a senior pair of magistrates were chosen to conduct the census.

Theoretically all these magistrates were chosen by the people at the popular assembly in the market- place (or in Maumbury Rings?). But the ordo recommended candidates to the people, and as the years passed the people's view became less and less important.

The prestige of office was great, but so were the expenses. If successful, you paid the bill for the election, and were expected to provide public entertainment, or build a temple, or aqueduct or statue at your own expense.

By the end of Roman Britain, citizens were reluctant to stand for office, and compulsion was introduced. Many decurions tried to move out of town to avoid it, something ultimately prohibited by decree.

THE PROVINCIAL COUNCIL

The ordo elected two representatives to the *concilium provinciae*, or provincial council, which met in London. At first sight this looks like a regional government advising the governor; but far from it. The governor was entirely autocratic and the provincial council met for formal purposes only, mainly connected with the Imperial cult, the worship of the emperor.

THE GOVERNOR

The governor kept his eye on what happened in Durnovaria through his own large civil service in London. The flow of paperwork from Dorset to London rivalled that of today, but none of it survives. The top men in the civil service were all seconded soldiers from the legions. Many grades of officials existed. In particular the *speculatores* (inspectors) travelled the province as personal representatives of the governor, and will often have been in Durnovaria. All over the country you would have found *Beneficiarii* or 'beneficiaries', who were in positions of trust, running post stations, organising taxes and otherwise representing the governor's interests.

TAXATION

The benefits, if such they were, of Roman life, had to be paid for. Every five years the census detailed people and property, and taxation was based on this. The *Procurator Augusti Britanniae* was responsible for the finances of the province, and under him other procurators had smaller areas of responsibility. One procurator of Britain, Classicianus, achieved fame by bringing to an end the slaughter following the rebellion of Boudica. (The procurator had a direct line of communication to the emperor.)

The Durotiges paid the three standard taxes to the tax contractors: the *annona*, or corn tax, to feed the army, the *tributum soli*, based on the productivity of the land, and the *tributum capitis* or poll tax. No doubt they paid up, reluctantly.

IV

THE TOWNS

DORCHESTER

Dorchester was called *Durnovaria* by the Romans. We are lucky to know this as it occurs in only one ancient document, the *Antonine Itinerary* (a third century route book). Most versions of the book actually spell it *Durnonovaria*, but one has *Durnovaria* and this is the name hallowed by use in modern times.

No one is sure what it means, except that the first part may refer to fist-sized pebbles.

The gates and many public buildings must have carried monumental inscriptions recording the name and other valuable information but alas, not one has survived; the only inscriptions are on an altar dedicated by a legionary centurion, a tombstone (see below) and a stamped tile. None of these name the town or the tribe.

The nearness of Maiden Castle and the later history of the town strongly suggest that Dorchester was the Roman capital of the Durotriges; but surprisingly this cannot be proved beyond doubt. Nowhere in the *Antonine Itinerary* is the name of the tribe attached to the name of the town — *Durnovaria Durotrigum* — as was normally done with tribal capitals. The only possible alternative is Ilchester *(Lindinis)* which also lies in Durotrigian territory. No one would seriously claim that it was the capital, but one curious piece of evidence makes it clear that Ilchester had some status.

In the museum at Chesters, a fort on Hadrian's Wall, are two inscribed construction stones from the Wall, recording the work of a construction gang provided by the Durotriges. The inscriptions read:

C DUROTRIGUM LINDINIESIS

This means the century (or perhaps civitas) of Durotriges from Lindinis.

It is unlikely that this means Ilchester was the capital, but it could mean that it was of equal status (by the fourth century); alternatively this stone was erected by the Ilchester gang, while another (lost) stone recorded the Dorchester gang. Certainly we must not underrate the importance of Ilchester.

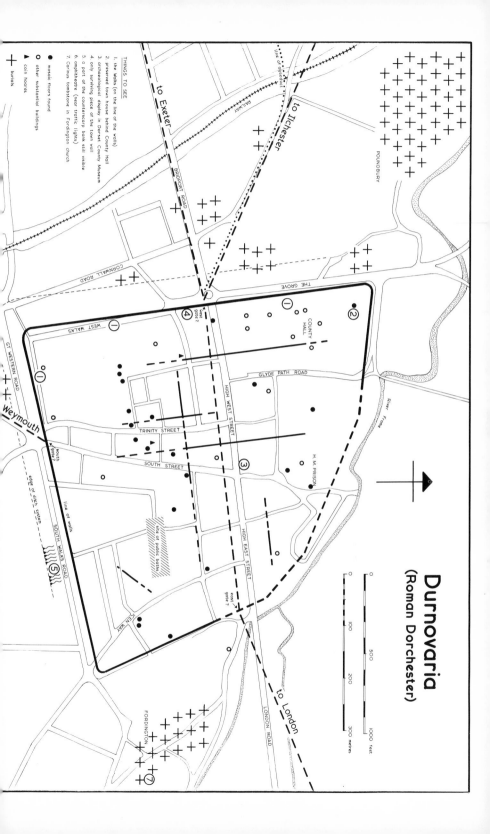

Durnovaria
(Roman Dorchester)

THINGS TO SEE

1. the Walks (on the line of the walls)
2. preserved town house behind County Hall
3. archaeological display in Dorset County Museum
4. only surviving piece of the town wall
5. a part of the counterscarp bank still visible
6. amphitheatre (near traffic lights)
7. Carinus tombstone in Fordington church

● mosaic floors found
○ other substantial buildings
▲ coin hoards
✝ burials

0   100   200   300 metres.
0   500   1000 feet.

to Exeter
to Ilchester
line of aqueduct
RAILWAY
BRIDPORT ROAD
CORNWALL ROAD
POUNDBURY
THE GROVE
WEST WALKS
west gate ?
① ②
COUNTY HALL
GLYDE PATH ROAD
River Frome
GT WESTERN ROAD
Weymouth
HIGH WEST STREET
③
TRINITY STREET
south gate ?
SOUTH STREET
H. M. PRISON
④
site of public baths
edge of ditch system
line of walls
SOUTH WALKS ROAD
⑤
KEN WAY
east gate ?
HIGH EAST STREET
to London
LONDON ROAD
FORDINGTON
⑦

The Romans were very good at persuading conquered tribes to accept the Roman way of life and to acquiesce in Roman rule. One of the ways in which this was done was by retaining the nominal 'independence' of the local tribe and gaining the support of their leaders through formal recognition of their position and other benefits. Once possessed of beautiful villas, steam baths and the other trappings of Roman civilisation, the princes of the Durotriges were scarcely likely to lead a movement advocating a rebellious return to the windswept hilltop of Maiden Castle!

It has even been suggested that the famous and magnificent Roman palace of Fishbourne, near Chichester, represents a direct reward to Cogidubnus, the pro-Roman chief of the Regnenses, and was used to entice the leaders of other tribes into Roman ways.

By and large, throughout the new province of Britannia, the Romans used the existing tribal groupings as the basis of their administrative divisions. Thus the Durotriges were made into a *civitas*. This is a word best left in Latin, as it means both the 'county' in geographical terms and the people themselves — a sort of 'county state'.

A civitas needed a civitas capital, and this was to be Dorchester. All over Britain tribal governments were moved from their draughty hillforts (or wherever they had been moved to since the invasion) down to lower ground, and usually to take over now disused army camps to provide their first temporary buildings. As we have seen in Chapter 2, this is probably what happened at Dorchester, though the original army camp has not been identified.

When did this happen? We know the general answer to this question: in his life of Agricola, governor of Britain from 77 to 84 AD, Tacitus writes that he encouraged the building of temples, markets and houses. Those towns with firm evidence for their beginnings, such as Cirencester, confirm that this was so. No doubt Dorchester was similar, though the evidence is not yet conclusive.

The governor would have appointed a *praefectus civitatis*, or civitas prefect, whose job was to advise the Durotrigian princes on the setting up of a Roman style town as their capital, and a system of government in line with that of Roman towns throughout the empire (see chapter 3).

No name can be put to a *praefectus civitatis* in Britain, but it is tempting to think that Carinus, whose tombstone records his Roman citizenship so proudly at an early date in the history of Dorchester, could originally have arrived as the prefect and stayed to settle. There is of course no way of proving or disproving such a hypothesis.

Though the governor provided encouragement and technical assistance (and no doubt compulsion if needed) the Durotriges had to pay for their own city. The Roman writer and philosopher Seneca is known to have lent 10,000,000 sesterces to British tribes to fund their Romanization programme.

The building of Dorchester must have been a financial strain, or else reluctantly undertaken; there is no sign of the elaborate and expensive public buildings being built at this date in richer cities like Verulamium. What wealth and splendour the Durotriges achieved in Dorchester and the surrounding villas seems to have come in the late third century, continuing till nearly the end of the fourth century.

But as the site of the fort is the major problem of the military phase of the town, so the nature of the early public buildings is the unanswered question about civilian Dorchester.

It may not have been as poor as we think. Excavations in Dorchester in the last 20 years have made one thing very clear; the builders of Saxon and medieval Dorchester used the Roman buildings as a quarry on a systematic and, for the archaeologist, devastating scale.

Time and time again all the archaeologists find of Roman buildings are the empty foundation trenches. Not only has all the dressed stone and brick from the walls gone, but the foundations have been quarried away to the last flint.

In these circumstances it is difficult to offer reliable opinions on the appearance of the town at various stages of its Roman history, and particular importance attaches to the rare sites where substantial parts of Roman buildings have been found. These include the very well preserved town house behind County Hall, and more significantly the sequence of buildings found at 34 Trinity Street; these ranged from simple timber buildings in the first century, timber framed buildings on stone foundations in the second, to a substantial stone and flint town house in the fourth.

The plan shows the little that we know of Roman Dorchester.

1. *The Walls*

Like most Roman towns in Britain the town was walled. The outline of the walls can clearly be seen from the air. Walls and ditches covered a swathe over 100 metres wide. This has dominated the pattern of town till Victorian times; not till then did the town spread outside.

The walls are best seen in the south west corner in Bowling Alley Walk. The wall stood on the edge of the grass verge. The bank which backed the wall (and contained the chalk from the ditches) extends across the path and some 20 metres into the hospital grounds. The triple ditches extended further south, the outer, southernmost, one being under the far side of Great Western road. Beyond that still, lay the counterscarp bank, under the houses on the south of the road. The scale of the work was enormous.

The ruined walls were cleared and the Walks constructed in the early eighteenth century, fortunately for us making a permanent marker of their route. Their position is clear on the west, south and southern part of the east side. Only on the north is their route uncertain where the building of the castle and later the prison, and possible erosion by the river has made it impossible to know what happened.

Only at a point just south of the Top o' Town roundabout does a fragment of walling survive. The facing stones have long since disappeared, but the core shows traces of the Roman style of building, with levelling courses of horizontal stones at intervals.

Imposing gates must have existed, on the west, south and east sides, but no trace has ever been found. Their positions can be calculated from the lines of the roads within the town, which are known in part from excavation. The roads do not by any means correspond with the modern streets.

One might expect the walls of a Roman town to be rectangular, as were those of a fort. But a glance at plans of towns in Roman Britain shows this was not so, and the reason is well understood.

At first the towns, with one or two exceptions, did not have walls. Under the *pax Romana* such things were unnecessary. Citizens were not allowed to carry arms.

But in 196 AD, the governor Clodius Albinus did something later

34

A photograph taken in about 1900 of the sole surviving fragment of the Roman wall of Dorchester. It is still visible, just south of the Top o' Town roundabout.

imitated by other governors of Britain. He declared himself Augustus and took the British legions to the continent to make himself emperor.

Before he went, he took steps to make it possible for the province to survive attack in his absence. The essential feature of Roman life and control was the towns, and he gave orders for them to be walled to protect themselves.

The towns enclosed the areas that had at that time been built upon, in the case of Dorchester about 30 hectares (75 acres). This is the reason for the irregular shape of the town.

An interesting discovery in excavations on the walls in Bowling Alley Walk, was that prior to the erection of the earliest earth and timber rampart, a start had been made on the foundations of a stone wall. This had got no further, when the presumably urgent construction of a massive (but quicker) earth bank buried it.

The walls did not finally gain a stone face till some time in the third century. (The date for this is very uncertain, and the date for the original construction is not beyond doubt.)

Many towns acquired bastions for artillery on the outer face of the walls in the fourth century. This may have happened at Dorchester, but there is no evidence for it.

Unlike many towns, Dorchester's walls do not seem to have been kept in repair in medieval times, and references to the walls in the borough records of the late fourteenth and fifteenth centuries clearly apply to earthworks rather than masonry structures.

35

2. Public Buildings

Nothing is known of the *forum* (market-place) and *basilica* (town hall), though some indication of its position near Cornhill can be gained from the plan of the internal roads of the town.

The *thermae* or heated baths (there may of course have been more than one) were partly excavated by the Central Excavation Unit of the Department of the Environment in 1977. They lay in the southeast quarter under the former rugby pitch of Hardye's Junior School at Wollaston House. After excavation they were reburied, and cannot be seen today.

The baths form the most substantial masonry remains of Roman buildings so far found in Dorchester. Though robbing of the stone had been extensive, the massive scale of the building ensured that some fragments of hypocausts and water tanks survived.

It is clear that the building covered an area at least 100m by 150m and must have been most impressive. It included several suites of the usual series of cold, tepid and hot rooms, and a large *palaestra*

A view of the 1977 excavations of the public baths of Roman Dorchester. Parts of several suites of heated rooms are visible, and prominent in the centre is a large laconicum or sauna.

(exercise yard) to the north.

The baths would have been one of the main social centres of the town and it is an indication of the depth of Romanization that such a very Roman feature should have flourished in this remote corner of the Roman empire.

3. *Maumbury Rings*

Outside the town on the road to the harbour at Weymouth, lay the amphitheatre. Maumbury Rings is a far cry from the Colosseum in Rome, but its function was basically similar.

We have already seen how it may have had a military use at

An aerial photograph of the Roman amphitheatre at Dorchester, Maumbury Rings. The Weymouth road in the top right corner lies on the route of the Roman road to Weymouth.

first, but certainly it was adapted to use for the town at an early date.

It was entirely built of earth and timber, and never rebuilt in stone. Perhaps Dorchester would never have had an amphitheatre had the military not been to hand; certainly it was no longer used by the mid-second century. Whether Christians were fed to the lions there, or gladiators fell in combat, is doubtful. Such shows were expensive to put on, and Durnovaria is unlikely to have supported them. But some form of entertainments must have occurred there, no doubt including wild beast shows, acrobats and other acts reminiscent of the modern circus. Perhaps these were a financial disaster, and this led to the abandonment.

Maumbury Rings started life as a Neolithic henge monument, the banks of which saved the Roman builders a considerable amount of earth moving as they adapted it. At the other end of of its history, it is interesting to note that it was fortified as an outpost by the Parliamentarians in the Civil War, and was equipped with anti-aircraft guns in World War II.

4. *The Aqueduct*

There is one feature of Roman towns where Dorchester has the best preserved example in the whole of Britain. This is the water supply aqueduct.

A constant supply of fresh, clean water was essential to a Roman town. The public baths used enormous quantities and filling their various pools and boilers from a well by buckets would have been almost impossible. Nevertheless the town had wells, and so would have had drinking water in emergency.

In and around Rome itself some 11 water channels brought water to the city from the surrounding hills on overhead masonry structures. Nothing as impressive (and expensive) as this existed at Dorchester. A single channel collected water from the Frome or one of its tributaries some distance from the town, and by keeping to a minimum gradient just managed to deliver it at ground level at the West gate.

It followed the contours, rather than cross low ground on masonry structures, and thus followed a very devious path. It can be seen at its best in Fordington Bottom, where the channel is still open, nearly at its original dimensions of about 2 metres wide and 1 metre deep.

At its source there will have been a dam. Where this was is unknown; Notton, near Maiden Newton, has been suggested. But it

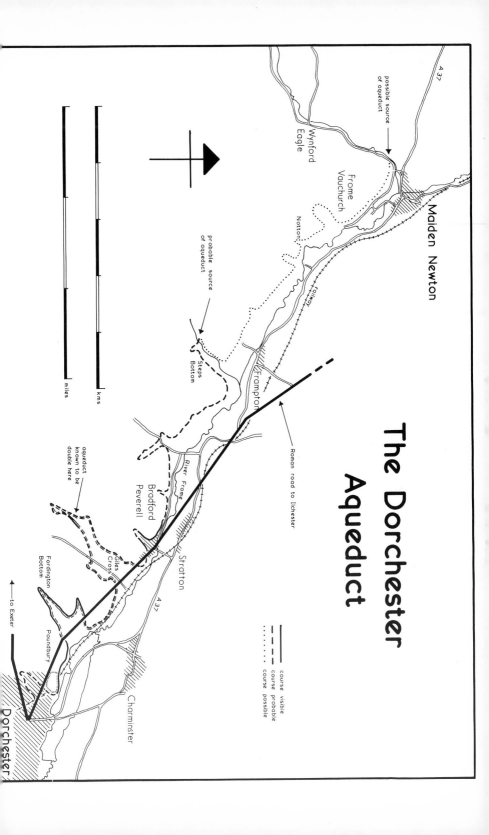

The Dorchester Aqueduct

miles

kms

Dorchester

to Exeter

A 37

Maiden Newton

Wynford Eagle

Frome Vauchurch

Notton

railway

Stratton

Bradford Peverell

River Frome

Frampton

Giles Cross

Fordington Bottom

Poundbury

Charminster

Steps Bottom

possible source of aqueduct

probable source of aqueduct

aqueduct known to be double here

Roman road to Ilchester

————— course visible
– – – – course probable
· · · · · · · course possible

The Roman aqueduct at Dorchester. Just above the railway the ground slopes steeply to the River Frome. All along this slope the course of the aqueduct can be seen.

is unlikely that the Frome itself would have been used, as this could not have been kept clean. It is more likely that it took its water from a small tributary, where the land use could have been controlled.

This means either the stream in Steps Bottom, near Frampton, or just possibly the spring at Wynford Eagle near Maiden Newton. Steps Bottom is most likely, as no firm evidence of the channel has ever been found further west than that. This would give a total channel length of about 9 miles.

A recent discovery is that a second, smaller, channel exists, just below the large one. Perhaps this was an early attempt which failed, or perhaps it served the military camp, as yet unlocated.

Near the west gate the aqueduct must have delivered its water to the *fons aquarum*, or public fountain. When new, the channel brought in some 25,000,000 gallons a day. Not all of this was used of course. Unlike a water main, an open channel cannot be switched off, so the surplus overflowed from the fountain, and was used to flush the lavatories before returning to the river below the town.

At the fountain the street mains began, and users like the baths would have had their own inlet; charges were based on the size of the inlet. Several of the timber water mains have been located besides streets in excavation; the wood has rotted, but the iron collars survive. Other mains would have been lead, but this rarely survives. No doubt every major house and establishment in the town was connected to the supply, and equally to the sewers.

There is no certain information on when the aqueduct was built or when it went out of use; linear features like this are notoriously difficult to date.

Some early accounts of the aqueduct describe it as a canal; but this is not meant to suggest it carried boats; it is far too small. Suggestions have recently been made that a canal for boats existed beneath the north walls of Durnovaria, and connected to the sea via navigable parts of the Frome. This is pure fantasy, and no archaeological evidence to support it exists.

Mosaic floor discovered in 1899 in Olga Road, Dorchester, set into the floor of the Victorian gallery of Dorset County Museum.

5. *The houses*

Roman towns, like modern ones, contained an enormous variety of houses and other buildings.

The decurions (see chapter 3) would have town houses of considerable splendour, with elaborate dining rooms, mosaic floors, formal gardens, and their own suite of baths. One of these was found in 1939 during excavations prior to the building of County Hall, and its remains are preserved on view.

There will have been many others, and some have been glimpsed at various times and their mosaic pavements lifted or reburied (two have been installed in the floor of the County Museum).

Other houses will have been smaller and poorer, and many artisans will have lived over their shops in crowded streets. But none of these have been excavated to date.

In the fringes of the town small scale industries existed (most Roman industries were small scale), and some of their workshops and furnaces have been seen on the County Hall site and under the Hospital. None of these are now on view.

6. *The cemeteries*

Around Durnovaria stretched the cemeteries, originally along the roads, but later filling in considerable areas between them.

Two areas have been extensively excavated: the area of the Poundbury industrial estate, and Fordington High Street.

At Poundbury excavations by Christopher Green over a number of years have revealed over 1,000 graves, their occupants rescued from the bulldozer constructing the industrial estate.

A majority belonged to the fourth century AD, a time when the Roman empire was officially Christian. They were buried on an east-west alignment and for the most part without grave goods. Family groups were in stone mausolea with paintings on the walls. Fragments of these give tantalising clues to the Christian ritual of the cemetery.

Most of the bodies were in wooden coffins, but the more important ones had lead linings, and a few were in hamstone coffins. Such coffins provide important evidence, as even hair may survive in such conditions.

The bones from Poundbury will, when analysed, give a substantial sample of the people of Durnovaria in the fourth century, with details of their size, appearance, diseases, and the other information which can now be obtained from such remains.

A historic photograph of the excavation in 1939 of the Roman town house in Colliton Park, at present on display behind County Hall.

In Fordington most burials were excavated in Victorian times, though there have been small excavations recently. Much of the village was covered by the cemetery. Here there was a greater variety of burial, ranging from the Christian to flexed burials which, though dating to the fourth century, reflected the burial pattern of the native Durotriges. There were also cremations, common in the Roman world in the first two centuries AD.

Most interesting of all is the one and only inscribed tombstone to be found, re-used in the porch of St George's, Fordington. This stone, found in 1907, can still be seen in the church at the west end. It is made of Purbeck marble, and would have been set in an ornamental surround, and brightly painted. Probably it would have been in the side of a small shrine or even mausoleum.

It is the only tombstone surviving; there can hardly have been a large number, unless the cemeteries were stripped of their stones (as in London) to provide emergency building materials in the last years of Roman Britain. Even then, it is surprising that more have not been found somewhere.

The stone belongs to the early years of the city, and must represent someone important. Unfortunately no indication is given of his function.

The stone, which is Purbeck marble, probably reads:

CARINO

CIVI.ROM

ANN.L

RUFINUS.ET

CARINA.ET

AVITA.FILI.EIUS

ET.ROMANA.UXOR

(In memory of) Carinus, Roman citizen, (died) aged 50 years. His children, Rufinus, Carina and Avita, with his wife Romana, (set up this memorial).

So we can put a name to these five inhabitants of earliest Dorchester. Clearly Carinus' Roman citizenship was of the greatest importance. There would not have been many such in Durnovaria in the first and second centuries.

Maybe he was a citizen from elsewhere in the empire who came on government business, came to love Dorset and stayed. He can hardly have been a Durotrigian native, as his name is not appropriate.

Rows of Christian graves in the Poundbury cemetery outside Dorchester. The site is now occupied by the industrial estate.

A bizarre Roman skeleton from the cemetery at Fordington. The woman's head has been removed after death and buried between her knees. There must be a reason of a magical or religious nature.

Lindinis was the second town of the Durotriges, as we know from the Hadrian's Wall inscriptions. It was smaller than Durnovaria, some 12 hectares (30 acres) in extent. We know even less about it, though excavations in recent years have begun to tell the story.

Today, of course, it is in Somerset, but it was certainly part of Dorset to its ancient inhabitants.

Ilchester was on the early Roman frontier, the Fosse Way. It is not surprising, therefore, to find it was originally a Roman fort site. The double-ditched defences of this have been located in several places, and its size may have been about 6 hectares (15 acres). Here the Fosse Way crossed the River Yeo, and this is the kind of site to be guarded by a fort.

It is interesting that the road from Dorchester does not appear to enter the fort gate, and this suggests that this road at least was only built when the civilian town began its life. In the case of Ilchester this seems to have been very late in the first century AD.

As in Dorchester, chance finds and excavations alike have produced indications of rich men's houses and other poorer buildings. Again the period of greatest prosperity seems to have been in the late third and fourth centuries.

OTHER SITES

Dorchester and Ilchester alone can be firmly regarded as towns. Other settlements existed (see chapter 7) and some may have been of considerable size. But it is doubtful if any were walled, and this is the usually accepted definition of a town.

Wareham, for instance, is a town where substantial finds of Roman pottery have been made, particularly in the north-west and south-east quarters. It is tempting to imagine a small town representing the trading headquarters of the various Roman industries of Purbeck, and it may have been so. But the evidence is slight, the walls were certainly built by King Alfred, and there is no known Roman road to connect it even to Dorchester.

V

ROMAN ROADS

Think of the Romans and their roads come first to mind. The Romans did not invent roads, as many of the preceding civilisations in the Middle East had them, but it was the Romans who developed them into the comprehensive system on which the administration of their empire depended. Naturally the system penetrated to Dorset.

Before the Romans came to Britain there were no roads at all, at least in the meaning of an engineered route with hard surface, foundations, drainage and bridges. There were of course trackways resulting from the passage of travellers; these trackways followed natural routes, and some of them, particularly the ridgeways, went for many miles. In some cases it seems that the Romans built roads which more or less followed the routes of these trackways.

The roads were one of the most drastic landscape changes that the Romans brought. All previous landscape features, even if manmade, were largely controlled by the presence of forests, rivers and hills. Now the route from A to B was in all probability a straight line drawn by an engineer on a map, and surveyed and carried out on the ground, initially at least, by the army. If your house unfortunately lay in its path, no planning permission or compulsory purchase order was needed for its destruction!

Initially the roads were built for military purposes; later they were adapted for the use of the new *civitates* and new ones built for the purpose.

It is usually difficult to date the construction of a road. In a town, features can be dated from pottery and coins in the buried layers; but once a road is out in the country miles of it might be excavated without finding anything to help date it. The only cases where it can be done with some certainty are those where a road clearly leads to the gate of a fort, rather than a town.

Alan Sorrell's reconstruction of the dramatic scene as the Roman army cuts the route of Ackling Dyke through the forests of Iron Age Dorset.

Roman roads were straight except where the terrain prevented it; if necessary they zig-zagged on steep descents and even performed long gentle curves.

Although visitors to Rome admire the Via Appia, constructed of lava blocks, and other similar paved roads, it must be remembered that the money for this sort of thing was rarely, if ever, available in Britain. British roads were of gravel (*via glareata* in Latin). There are just one or two possible cases of a paved road, and even these are doubtful.

Fine gravel as a running surface lay over larger stones forming a foundation. At each side lay a drainage ditch, and the road itself was normally carried on a causeway which can in some cases be surprisingly high (particularly Ackling Dyke); nevertheless the reason was the same, namely drainage. Nothing destroys a road faster than lying water and frost. In hollows, culverts carried surface water or streams beneath the road.

The roads were surprisingly narrow; although the causeway (or *agger*) may have been as much as 20 metres in width, the running surface at its top was rarely more than 3 metres (10 feet) wide. This was just enough for two vehicles moving slowly to pass. When traffic ruts survive, they are normally central on the road. Once a road has been ploughed over it gives the appearance of having been much wider; but this is unlikely to have been so.

Where streams were substantial, bridges were built, sometimes of stone, sometimes of timber. But if the stream was unlikely to hinder traffic, then a ford was often enough. No Roman bridge survives in Britain, in spite of many traditions to this effect. Normally rivers have eaten away even the foundations, and roads usually disappear as they enter a river's flood plain. Some idea of what the bridges looked like can be got from surviving examples on the continent, and from the foundations of bridges on Hadrian's Wall at Chesters and Willowford.

NAMES AND MILESTONES

Roman roads carried names, and usually commemorated the name of the consul or emperor under whom construction or repair was carried out. No milestones survive in Dorset but an uninscribed stone outside Dorchester (708913) might just be a worn example. Responsibility for maintenance, which initially was carried out by the army, was transferred to the local communities as soon as possible.

Three routes are known for certain in Dorset, and they are described below. Some others have been claimed, but not proved. There may well have been minor routes, particularly to the industries of Purbeck, but these are not likely to have been constructed in the grand manner of Ackling Dyke, and very little trace survives.

1. *Ackling Dyke* (Old Sarum — Badbury — Dorchester — Exeter)

This is the main road of Roman Dorset, beyond question. Ultimately it came from London, via Staines, Silchester (near Reading) and Old Sarum (near Salisbury). The road passes through Dorset *en route* to Exeter.

From about 55 AD till the late 60's the second Augustan Legion had its headquarters at Exeter (Isca). As it is difficult to imagine the legion being without reliable communications to London, it seems very likely that this road was military in origin, adapted later for use by the *civitates* of the Durotriges and the Dumnonii (of Devon) whose new capitals in any case lay on its route. If so, and it is not

Ackling Dyke at Badbury Rings. The road runs bottom left to top right, just touching the hillfort ramparts. In the field in the foreground it crosses the road from Lake Farm towards Bath.

beyond doubt, then it was built in its very impressive style right from the start, as excavations (see below) have shown no trace of a more modest construction buried beneath it. It must not be forgotten that the Roman forts at Hod Hill and Waddon Hill are on no known part of the road system at all.

Ackling Dyke enters modern Dorset at Bokerley Junction, where it passes through Bokerley Dyke (SU 033198). From here it runs straight to Badbury Rings near Wimborne, with one very small change in alignment near Gussage St Michael. Most of the stretch from Gussage to the border can be walked, and is one of the most magnificent stretches of undamaged Roman road in Britain.

At Badbury there is a complex road junction. Originally it seems that the road from London swung southeast to the fortress at Wimborne (route 2), but from the building of the Exeter fortresss the main road must have swung south-west towards Dorchester. This stretch too has one slight change of direction, east of West Kingston. It is interesting to speculate whether this and the similar bend at Gussage St Michael reflect slight inaccuracies in surveying, or whether they avoid obstacles we are unaware of. In Puddletown Forest (735923) there is a sharp S-bend in the road; the reason is clear, the road negotiates a steep slope and changes direction temporarily to ease the gradient.

From Dorchester the road is much less straight, climbing soon after it leaves the town onto a ridge where it may have followed a prehistoric route. There are many short changes of direction. Near Eggardon Hillfort the road leaves the chalk high ground and drops onto the greensand, with its many small hills and valleys.

Here its route must have been tortuous, and tracing it is very difficult. There is sufficient evidence to suggest that it passed through or near Bridport, Chideock, Morecombe Lake, Charmouth and Pen Cross, before leaving Dorset at Raymond's Hill (SY329963). Its route does not become entirely clear again till it reaches Axminster.

Excavations on Roman roads tend to produce very little information, especially where the road has been reduced by ploughing. But two excavations have been carried out by the Dorset Institute of Higher Education on Ackling Dyke, at points where it is in perfect condition, and give an indication of what it was like when it was built.

One was in Thorncombe Wood (727920), and one near Eggardon hillfort; the excavations produced almost identical cross sections.

In Thorncombe Wood the road is on sand and gravel, and its *agger* is built of gravel dug from pits close to the road. The causeway is 8m wide at the base, narrowing at the top to a little over 3m (10ft). Central ruts were still visible on the surface.

At Eggardon (544937) the materials of the road were entirely different. Here it lies on the chalk, and the causeway is entirely of flint, quarried from the chalk nearby. The sloping sides were of chalk rubble (also from the quarries) but the running surface was of gravel clearly brought from some distance away, perhaps on Black Down near Portesham.

2. *Hamworthy — Wimborne — Bath*

It is quite certain that this route originated early in the invasion. The road runs from Hamworthy (at about 002904) where finds strongly suggest an invasion harbour. From here it runs almost due north to Lake Farm, Wimborne, where a large base of the second Augustan legion existed (see chapter 2).

The road turned north-west from here to reach the road junction at Badbury Rings. Since the Lake Farm site only existed during the invasion period, it follows that the road was built to bring supplies ashore.

From Badbury Rings the road ran across country towards Bath. It is difficult to follow once it leaves Dorset and the chalk near Ashmore (922175), but it is heading for the Bath area and perhaps the early harbour at Sea Mills. It is tempting to visualise heavy equipment from Lake Farm moving towards the Bristol Channel from here as the campaigning area moved farther north.

3. *Weymouth — Dorchester — Ilchester*

Another harbour road runs from Weymouth to Dorchester. It has a suspected military origin, but by no means as clear as that of route 2.

The point of origin in Weymouth is quite uncertain, in spite of the tradition that it was at the village of Radipole. Firstly the coastline and sea levels have changed drastically since Roman times, making it difficult to establish the nature of the Backwater and the river Wey in the first century AD. Secondly, although some finds have been made at Radipole, these only reflect settlement and not necessarily a harbour; finds have equally come from elsewhere, including some from the Backwater itself, near the gasholder. Thirdly, the road itself cannot be traced further south than the ridgeway, and so leaves its destination uncertain.

Nevertheless, there must have been a harbour somewhere on the Backwater or the Wey. Once the road crosses the ridgeway its route becomes clear, as it now forms the A354 to Dorchester. The route is actually that of the Turnpike road, but when trenches are cut in the adjacent fields the side ditches of the preceding Roman road can be seen.

From Dorchester the road leaves by the west gate (there is no evidence of a north gate) and almost immediately leaves the Exeter road and heads north-west. After three miles it crosses the Frome Valley between Bradford Peverell and Stratton (the latter name indicating the presence of a "street"). In these three miles there must have been five bridges over the aqueduct (see chapter 4). From here the road turned to a more northerly direction, and for the most part lies under the modern A37. It can however be seen following an independent route at Hyde House (near Frampton), at Holywell (near Evershot) and just to the east of Melbury Park. It leaves the county near Ryme Intrinseca at (572100) on its way to Ilchester.

Whether this section of route 3 had a military origin or not is unclear. At Ilchester it does not appear to enter the gates of the fort, and it may have been built to connect the two towns of the Durotriges.

VI
THE VILLAS

The main sign of Romanization in the Dorset countryside was the appearance of villas. There is not much evidence for them in the first and second centuries AD, but in the third and fourth they began to be built in greater numbers, and towards the end of Roman rule in Britain some were both large and luxurious.

The Latin word *villa* means farm and implies that it is a substantial establishment with a farmhouse built to a considerable degree of luxury. Some of the villas near Rome itself were little short of palaces. While in smaller ones the farmyard was right in front of the house, in the larger villas farming activities were carried out round the back, and the main courtyard became a formal garden.

In Dorset, many of them represented the country homes of the native Durotrigian nobility, who would also have had a luxury house in town. The wealth needed to build them came from farming, from ownership of land, and from whatever industries the nobility had their money invested in.

The wealth shown by the villas in the fourth century would seem to imply that the Durotriges, or at least their leaders, had become very prosperous by then. It is a little difficult to see where this prosperity came from, and because of this some historians have suggested that the explanation lies in the arrival of men and their money from Gaul. Britain, particularly the west, may have seemed a haven from political troubles and Saxon attacks, and rich nobles of the tribes in Gaul may have bought up modest Durotrigian villas with their land, and modernised them. This is certainly a possible explanation, but at present, there is not enough evidence to decide.

The villas in Durotrigian territory are in two main groups; those around Ilchester (numerous, but mostly in Somerset now) and those around Dorchester. It is unusual to find large villas more than an hour or so on horseback from a town, but there were a few, such as Tarrant Hinton. These may have had special functions, such as the home of a procurator in charge of an imperial estate of some sort.

The villas of Dorset have suffered much damage over the centuries. Most were abandoned by their owners around 400 AD when growing economic and political chaos made it impossible to maintain them. Danger of attack (a possibility in Dorset, though a near certainty in many eastern parts of the province) persuaded owners to live in town and probably to transport their harvest there as soon as possible. Dorchester and Ilchester at least had walls to defend them.

The villas then suffered what every abandoned house suffers, ranging from small boys with catapults breaking the windows, to large scale digging in medieval times to find dressed stone to use in a new church. Often little but the mosaic floors survives; the floors are useless for building material, unless of course they lie over a hypocaust, or underfloor heating system. In such cases they may well have been torn up to get at the large slabs which carried them over the heating channels.

In the end the villas became slight bumps in the ground. Nevertheless, the discovery of a mosaic floor belonging to a ruined villa still provides one of the most exciting moments in archaeology as the pictures and patterns of a bygone age are uncovered. If you are fortunate enough to make such a discovery by accident, please get expert help from Dorset County Museum rather than attempt to uncover it yourself. The remains are normally very fragile indeed.

A more recent hazard for villas has been inexpert excavation by eighteenth and nineteenth century antiquarians, which has left us details of mosaic floors and little else. The mosaics are a tiny, though fascinating, part of the story. Nowadays equal attention is paid to the farm buildings and the evidence for farming, in order to build up a portrait of the people and how they lived and worked.

In fact a newly discovered villa site, which has not been 'excavated' in recent centuries is a valuable find indeed, and there is a strong case for the purchase and preservation of the site under permanent grassland, so that at some future date more advanced archaeological techniques can be brought to bear. In these circumstances the site would need protection, not only from the plough, but also from treasure hunters who, in spite of the Ancient Monuments and Archaeological Areas Act of 1979, which makes it an offence, continue to damage scheduled sites throughout Britain.

FRAMPTON

In the water meadows beside the Frome at Frampton lies one of the earliest villas to be discovered in Dorset. Found in 1796, its mosaic floors were cleared and drawn by Lysons. Its main interest lies in the Christian symbol, found in the floor pattern (see chapter 8). The floor was almost certainly laid in the fourth century. Almost nothing else is known about the house and its farm. Today there is nothing to see but an area of rubble surrounded by the artificial channels of the water meadows, which will have severely damaged the remaining parts of the villa. It is doubtful whether the pavements still survive under the soil.

HINTON ST MARY

Hinton St Mary is the most famous of the Dorset villas. It was discovered by accident in 1963 when the village blacksmith was digging a hole for his wife's washing line! Oddly enough the villa suffered a similar fate to Frampton; we now know little more about it than can be deduced from the mosaic. This time the reason was the enormous publicity which followed the discovery, making further archaeological research difficult.

The publicity came from the fact that the mosaic floor had at its centre a picture of the head and shoulders of Christ. This is discussed in chapter 8. The floor was bought by the British Museum, and forms a major exhibit in its Romano-British display. Also on display is the complete iron grille from one of the villa's windows. As at Frampton, there is nothing to see at the site today.

TARRANT HINTON

A large villa at Tarrant Hinton has been under excavation since 1968. Spectacular mosaics have not survived here, and the villa lies in close proximity to a considerable area of Romano-British settlement. It may not be the same sort of country house as the other villas described here. Its most spectacular finds have been a twin-cylinder pump from its well, and an inscription on a sandstone block, also thrown into the well.

The inscription is important, as inscriptions from villas are very rare indeed. It is a tombstone from the cemetery belonging to the villa or the settlement. It reads:

CUP VEP DECESSIT ANNO XXXVIIII TUSCO
ET BASSO COS VII KAL SEPTEMB
Cupitius Vep . . . died in his 39th year in the consulship of
Tuscus and Bassus, on the 26th August'.

Mentioning the names of the consuls is a common method of naming the year, in this case 258 AD. Although the inscription mentions September, the date is actually in August, because Roman dates are given as so many days before certain fixed points in the month (in this case seven days, counting inclusively, before the 1st of September).

Most interesting of all is the second name, or cognomen; beginning with Vep . . . it is most likely to be Celtic rather than Roman. Thus it is possible that Vep . . . is the only Romano-British Durotrigian native to whom we can put a name, or at least part of one! He could, however, have come from any other Celtic tribe.

The pump is of great interest. Made of a wooden block, with bronze and lead working parts, it may have been worked by slaves or a treadmill to pump water from the well. Such items of engineering were common enough in the Roman world, but their survival is rare.

HALSTOCK

At Halstock a very large courtyard villa (of the group attached to Ilchester) has been under excavation by a series of excavators since 1967. The excavations, in difficult conditions on a wet clay soil, have produced spectacular baths, and some of the barns and other farm buildings. The main courtyard house has sadly been ploughed well below the level of its floors so that knowledge of large parts of the

villa is confined to the ground plan given by the foundations.

At the time of writing both Tarrant Hinton and Halstock are still under excavation in the summer, and volunteers can be put in touch with the excavators by Wimborne and Dorset County Museums respectively.

DEWLISH

For eleven years from 1968 to 1979 the villa at Dewlish (near Puddletown) was the training excavation of the Dorset Institute of Higher Education (formerly the Weymouth College of Education).

The site in the grounds of Dewlish House has a complex history. The dry summer of 1976 revealed many features in parchmarks in the grass. The earlist occupation was a very wide scatter of Mesolithic flints dating to about 6,000 BC. There is a farm of Iron Age date (not excavated) with its many grain storage pits and field enclosures. This was followed by small square 'Celtic' fields of the early part of the Roman period; but no trace of the farm of this date was found, and it is impossible to say whether it was a villa.

A reconstruction by Peter Woodward of the landscape around the Dewlish villa in the fourth century AD.

Dewlish Roman Villa; excavation of the entrance passage with its key pattern mosaic. The holes in the floor were made by fence posts in recent times.

Dewlish Roman Villa; the moment of discovery of the mosaic floor of room 11 (the dining room).

Dewlish Roman Villa; the sole surviving fragment of the mosaic from the main part of room 11. A leopard is killing a gazelle, suggesting that the theme of the rest of the floor was hunting.

Dewlish Roman Villa; fragment of the floor of the changing room of the bath suite. Cupid (upside down in the bottom right of the picture) leads a procession of fantastic sea creatures including a ram, a leopard and a dolphin, around the room. In the centre, but destroyed, was probably a picture of Neptune, god of the sea.

Then in the late third century AD the field banks were levelled and a small farm was built, just about qualifying as a villa. A single long building housed the owner at one end and the barn at the other. There were no mosaics, but the walls were plastered and painted.

Early in the fourth century these early buildings were converted entirely into enlarged farm buildings, and a larger luxury house was built on a second side of the courtyard, with a full length veranda and central porch. But still the floors were wooden or rammed earth.

After a short life the villa was abandoned and allowed to fall down in part. Whether the same fate befell the farm is not clear, but it is unlikely.

Then in the second half of the fourth century either prosperity returned or, more likely, the property was bought for renovation. The house was rebuilt, in some parts from the foundations up. The farm buildings were cleared away entirely, and in their place appeared a small temple and priest's house. The villa had become a small pagan religious settlement.

The baths were enlarged — perhaps healing was a central feature of the cult — and almost every room in the main building was fitted with mosaic floors. At the back a huge kitchen block was built, presumably to cope with the visitors.

Success did not last long; by about 400 the building was in ruins again, though the farming no doubt continued. But the farm buildings associated with the grand phase of the villa were clearly on another site and have not been found.

How far the history of Dewlish villa is typical, remains to be seen.

The house was well preserved in places. Some of the mosaics were reburied, some vulnerable fragments were taken up by Dorset County Museum. The leopard and gazelle fragment hangs in Dewlish House. Fragments of two successive floors of the baths changing room hang in the entrance hall of Dorset County Museum. These show an interesting change of fashion in floor patterns, from abstract geometric patterns, to a frieze of fantastic sea creatures swimming round King Neptune, led by the god Cupid.

Unfortunately the early farm buildings and the temple complex which replaced them had been ploughed away to their foundations, and little is known of upper parts of the buildings.

Nothing of the villa is to be seen at Dewlish today, as the site has been filled in and re-seeded.

VII
THE COUNTRYSIDE

Archaeologists once used to imagine the Romano-British countryside as some sort of idyllic parkland with a splendid villa glimpsed through the trees every few miles. It is now realised that in the later years of Roman Britain the population had almost certainly risen to a level which was only to be reached again at the time of the Industrial Revolution. In fact one of the most tragic results of the end of Roman Britain is that the population dropped to a fraction of its former number; a process that almost certainly involved a great deal of misery.

It is very difficult to calculate populations at remote periods in history. The Romans held a regular census of course, but the records do not survive. The only way to achieve an estimate is to look at two things; the size and number of towns, and any countryside areas where we have a complete sample of the population density.

In some areas of fenland in Lincolnshire, aerial photography has shown that newly settled land maintained small settlements at intervals of less than 1 kilometre. Nearer Dorset, the route of the M5 was carefully studied in advance of the building of the motorway, giving a linear sample across Gloucestershire and Somerset. As in Lincolnshire Roman settlements were found to exist much more frequently than had been imagined. In many parts of the country which are sparsely inhabited today, such as the chalk downs in Wessex, settlements abounded.

The result is a current estimate of population of over 5 million, a considerable increase on a probable Iron Age population of 1 million.

What caused this population explosion? Farming methods were improved by the introduction of Roman technology, though this is one of the most difficult topics to investigate. More importantly there was a large military and civil market for food which encouraged (or rather demanded) an increase in production. Finally, and most significant of all, the *pax Romana*, or Roman peace, meant that many generations lived their lives in peace without regular warfare to reduce their numbers and ruin agriculture.

As the numbers increased, new settlements sprang up and more and more land was taken into cultivation. In the fens of eastern

A corn drier in the barn at Halstock, near Yeovil. A heated floor dried the grain before storage.

England Roman water engineering made possible the draining and reclamation of large areas of land which were then intensively settled. In Dorset it is doubtful whether any substantial tract of land remained unsettled. In fact the supply of timber for fuel and construction work must have been a major problem for the Durotrigian administrators.

Settlement in Dorset was enormously varied. There were the villas occupying the choicest positions and some of the best land. There were farms, large and small, of less than villa status. There were hamlets consisting of several farms grouped together. There were small villages and large villages. In fact, a similar variety of settlement existed to that of today with, of course, a much larger percentage of the population living in the country.

The formal changes brought about by the Romans centred mainly on the towns. Only gradually did the effects reach the countryside. A Durotrigian farmer continued to live as his ancestors had; his house was round, built of timber and thatched. His fields were small, the size that could be ploughed in a day. (His fields can still be seen in many places — they are referred to by archaeologists as 'Celtic' fields.)

He grew spelt (a primitive form of wheat), and kept the usual domesticated animals; sheep, goats, pigs and cattle. At all times and places in Roman Britain mixed farming was the rule, as it has continued to be till very recent times.

Gradually changes came about. The pottery bought in Dorchester changed shape because it was primarily made for the military market. The farmer could buy more of it, as the new towns and the army provided a profitable market for his produce even after taxation.

New crops were introduced, including rye, oats, vetch and flax. In addition there was cabbage, parsnip, turnip, carrot and other vegetables. In favourable areas fruit trees were grown including the vine, plum, apple, mulberry and walnut. Wine was the Roman drink, but it never entirely replaced beer drinking in Britain. Wine must have been made in Dorset but, as now, found it difficult to compete with wine from more favourable growing areas on the continent.

The farmer's house might have stayed as it was, round huts are found throughout Roman Britain. But where Roman influence was stronger, houses were gradually rebuilt in Roman style. The critical change was to a rectangular shape; with it came tiled roofs and painted and plastered walls.

The best known Roman village site in Dorset is Meriden Down near Winterbourne Houghton. Like many such villages it lies not in the valley with the later medieval villages, but on a chalk spur of comparatively high ground. It occupies nearly 2 hectares. Like a deserted medieval village it includes platforms representing ruined houses (some rectangular, some circular), working areas and small enclosures.

Interestingly, the houses lie centrally in an area cut off by fences from the surrounding fields. Rather than the houses surrounding the village green, the green surrounds the houses.

But other villages are different, and every imaginable shape

At Turnworth, preserved in parkland, a Romano-British farm (centre left) lies in the traces of its fields and lanes. The low sun makes these faint banks visible to the aerial camera.

occurs, including long streets with houses either side, and houses clustered round what looks almost like a village green.

The villages which survive unploughed as earthworks are rare and valuable. Meriden Down and Grimstone (near Dorchester) and a few others hold many secrets of the Dorset countryside in Roman times and deserve major and intensive investigation. In the meantime they must be protected from damage as carefully as more spectacular monuments.

One of the few excavated hamlets is at Studland on Poole Harbour. Here buildings dated from the conquest to the end of the Roman period. Round huts were succeeded on the same sites by roughly rectangular huts measuring about 12m by 7m. These were still of wattle and daub, but had substantial stone foundations. They were rebuilt many times, but basically were 'long-houses' where the family lived in one end and the animals in the other. This was the form of the original farm building at the Dewlish villa site, but there further development took place.

It is often said that life in the countryside changed little from Iron

Smacam Down near Cerne Abbas. The whole landscape is covered with the pattern of small fields characteristic of farming in the Iron Age and Roman periods. A small farm lies in the bushes a little right of centre.

Age times. But this cannot be true within the boundaries of the Roman province. No doubt the Durotrigian farmer grumbled, but he lived at peace most of the time, had a larger family, fed them well, sold his produce profitably in the markets and bought himself some of the trappings of Roman civilisation in the form of clothes and ornaments. His house became rectangular, perhaps roofed in tile, distinctly drier and more comfortable. No longer was it necessary to bury the corn in the ground to preserve it, and he learnt (especially if he was close to one of the more Romanized villa estates) to dry his corn in kilns and keep it in granaries.

Some suggestion has been made that the villa estates, especially in the south-west, changed the ancient landscape of Celtic fields and made their profits from large scale sheep farming. Certainly at the Dewlish villa small fields next to the house appear to have been obliterated and open parkland created. But at other villas where environmental evidence shows what farming operations were going on, it is clear that most of the activities of traditional mixed farming were undertaken.

VIII
RELIGION

The Roman world had many religions, and for the first three centuries AD any religion was tolerated by government provided it obeyed the rules. This meant that it had to allow for the deity of the emperor, and this presented little if any difficulty to the many gods of the Greek and Roman Pantheon (see below).

Christianity of course could not allow the deity of the emperor, and this led to the persecution of Christians, particularly under Nero and Diocletian. But Christianity was a very different religion to most of the others.

Following the conversion of the emperor Constantine in 312 AD, Christianity became the official and required faith of the empire. Some of the other religions suffered repression in their turn, but many continued to flourish in far off corners of the empire.

THE PANTHEON

Until the spread of Christianity, most Romans (and the Greeks before them) worshipped the many and varied gods of the Pantheon. This is difficult for us to understand, since a traditional Roman god was completely unlike the Christian idea of God.

The gods (note the plural) were simply a superhuman race, giant in stature, immortal, and living on Mount Olympus or other magical and inaccessible locations. They lived their own lives and obeyed no moral rules in doing so. They fought, stole and went to bed with the wrong partners. Jupiter was their king, and Juno their queen. They all had special attributes, for example Mars, god of war, and Venus, goddess of love and beauty. The gods were not necessarily concerned with human life at all; they just carried on with their own affairs.

But, of course, they were all powerful and could if they wished intervene in human life to considerable effect. Thus it was that enormous sums of money were expended both at public and private level to catch the interest of a god and persuade him or her to intervene in human life.

An artist's reconstruction of an open air sacrifice before the temple at Maiden Castle.

This was done by the provision of temples, expensive and attractive buildings, which provide some of the very best examples of classical architecture; the Parthenon in Athens was simply the home provided by the Athenians for their patron goddess Athene.

You hoped that the god would find your temple irresistibly attractive and reside there. The temple was the god's home and no one was allowed in except the priest or priestess. Assemblies of people, if they happened at all, occurred around an outdoor altar in front of the temple.

Grand ceremonies were carried out at state level, and at a personal level you attracted the god's attention by making offerings of small cakes, wine, small animals, a bull — the more expensive, the more likely to succeed! Food offerings were consumed by the priests on the god's behalf.

Excavations of temples always produce examples of this process, since the wealthy, when successful, recorded their offerings on stone altars which can still be read. The best instance in the province of Britain is at Bath where Sulis, goddess of the hot spring, was worshipped. In the days of primitive medicine those gods which offered healing were most successful in financial terms; this accounts for the great wealth of the buildings in the temple complex at Bath.

DORSET

When the Romans came to Britain they found many gods being worshipped in a similar way to their own. This presented no problem; the gods carried on, and in many cases were declared to be identical with particular Roman gods. For instance Sulis at Bath was equated with Minerva, and is addressed on some inscriptions by the double name.

The only exception was the religion of the Druids. This, we are told, involved human sacrifice and other unmentionable horrors. Druidism was forbidden and the historian Tacitus gives a graphic description of the violent destruction of the priests and their sacred groves on Anglesey.

We do not know if the Druids operated among the Durotriges, though it is likely enough. But it is almost certain that throughout Dorset local gods existed in a style very similar to the Roman gods; and these would have been worshipped at magical spots such as forests and springs. By the spring at Cerne Abbas is the huge chalk figure of a fertility god; perhaps in the Cerne Giant we can actually

A votive bronze bull with human busts attached found in the temple at Maiden Castle. It may represent some aspect of the god worshipped there.

see a picture of a native Durotrigian god, as assimilated into the Roman system.

No doubt with Roman names as well as their own, these gods continued to be worshipped in the countryside. In the towns there will have been greater pressure for allegiance to be transferred to the Roman gods themselves. As we shall see, many of these native gods staged a comeback in the later years of Roman Britain.

CHRISTIANITY

Neither Dorchester nor Ilchester has yet produced a single temple to any god, native or Roman, though no doubt they existed. Oddly enough it is the countryside which has given us some very spectacular evidence. In two Dorset villas the mosaic floors of the main reception-cum-dining room *(triclinium)* contain one of the symbols of

71

Christianity. This was the logo formed from the Greek letters chi and rho, which together represent chr, the first letters of Christ's name.

At Frampton villa, 5 miles west of Dorchester in the valley of the Frome, the main pavement featured figures from classical mythology, including Cupid, Neptune, and the story of Bellerephon and the Chimaera. Neptune and Cupid are honoured in lines of verse set into the floor.

But very oddly the dining apse opening from the main room has on its threshold three floral whorls on either side of a roundel containing the chi-rho symbol.

It raises intriguing but unanswerable questions. Was the owner Christian? If so, what is Neptune doing so prominently elsewhere on the floor? Was the side-room used as a Christian chapel and its use symbolised in the floor as you entered? Perhaps Neptune and the other ancient gods were regarded as mere figures of mythology, not seen to be in conflict with Christianity?

Nevertheless in several parts of the room pictures of mythological scenes have at some time been hacked from the floor, and this may be the work of Christians who felt they were inappropriate.

At Hinton St Mary near Sturminster Newton, the pictures are less equivocal. Bellerophon and the Chimaera appear in the apse, but the central panel in the main room shows the head and shoulders of a man; behind him is the chi-rho symbol, and on either side pomegranates, symbols of eternal life. There is very little doubt that this is meant to be Christ.

As such it is a floor of the greatest importance, and it is not surprising that it is now to be seen in the British Museum. (Frampton is buried again, and may have been severely damaged by the construction of water meadows.)

These mosaic floors, taken together with evidence from Dorchester at least confirm that in the 4th century AD Christianity had come to Dorset, and was probably widespread.

In the cemetery at Poundbury outside Dorchester upwards of 1,000 burials were found, aligned in Christian fashion and the bodies fully extended on their backs. The manner of burial coupled with the

Hinton St Mary villa. The floor of the dining room, now in the British Museum. Perhaps the most famous mosaic in Britain because of the figure in the centre of the lower part of the floor; this is almost certainly Christ since the chi-rho symbol lies behind the head and it is flanked by pomegranates, symbols of eternal life.

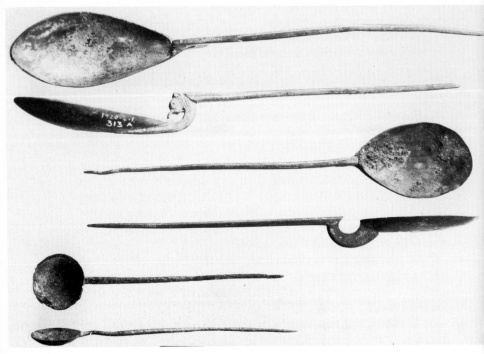

Silver spoons found in Somerleigh Court in Dorchester. These may have been used in Christian ritual as one has a fish drawn in the bowl and another a Christian inscription.

absence of grave goods, and the occasional find of a chi-rho coin pierced for wearing round the neck, indicate that this was one of the burial places of the Christian community in Durnovaria.

There must have been a church, similar to the small one known from Silchester. Moreover, in the Poundbury cemetery among the graves were several mausolea. In one of these fragments of painted wall decoration show rows of officials with staffs of office, perhaps church elders. The decoration includes one chi-rho.

Other finds from Dorset confirm the practice of Christianity. These include two silver rings from the villa at Fifehead Neville with chi-rho on the bezel, and a group of silver spoons found at Somerleigh Court in Dorchester. One of these has a fish depicted on the bowl, and another the message 'Augustine vivas'; both indicating Christian use. The spoons, found with 50 silver coins, may well have been part of the ritual of the Dorchester church, buried in some emergency and never recovered.

74

The Cerne Giant. This fertility god, carved in the chalk hillside, probably dates from the Roman period. He may well be a native god equated with the Roman god Hercules.

The major evidence for the revival of pagan religion at the end of the Roman period lies in two Romano-Celtic temples, one at Maiden Castle and the other at Jordan Hill, near Weymouth.

Jordan Hill is much damaged and badly excavated; its identity is not entirely certain. But the Maiden Castle temple was excavated by Wheeler, and a full account can be read in his report on the hillfort.

The temple consisted of a square *cella* or shrine, surrounded by a square portico. This was the usual shape in the third and fourth centuries for temples of native gods, as distinct from the classical Roman ones, who are more likely to have had classical temples.

Beside the Maiden Castle temple lay a small two-roomed house, presumably for the priest. There is some evidence that all the eastern end of the hillfort was walled off to form the temple precinct. It seems to have been reasonably prosperous, but we have no means of knowing the name of the god.

Most interesting of all is the fact that below the ruins of the temple (which can still be seen) Wheeler found a small wooden hut from the hillfort of 400 years before the temple, and this hut may itself have been a shrine. It is possible that one of the gods of the Durotriges worshipped in the old hillfort had retained his identity, to benefit from a pagan revival in the late fourth century.

Certainly there was a pagan revival at this time and one wonders what the Christian community thought of it. In some parts of Britain such temples became extremely prosperous and the best known example is at Lydney in Gloucestershire, also excavated by Wheeler.

At the villa at Dewlish (see chapter 6) the late fourth century saw the building of a small square temple and an attendant house; this too may have been for a Celtic god, but heavy ploughing has removed any certain evidence.

IX

TRADE AND INDUSTRY

One of the attractions which brought the Romans to Britain was the prospect of profits from a variety of industries. The first century geographer Strabo described pre-Roman Britain as exporting gold, silver, iron, slaves, corn, cattle, hides and hunting dogs.

Mines for the various metals were the personal property of the emperor and run for his private profit by procurators. These mines provided some of the few instances in Roman Britain where industry operated on the large, messy scale more familiar to us from the Industrial Revolution. The most famous of these is perhaps the gold mine at Dolaucothi in Central Wales, with its seven aqueducts supplying water power.

Similar scenes could be found at the lead and silver mines of Charterhouse, the tin mines of Cornwall, the iron mines of the Weald, and other mining centres.

No metal was mined in Dorset, but there were two major and no doubt profitable industries; stone and pottery. The pottery industry was almost certainly in private Durotrigian hands, while the stone industries may have had local or just possibly imperial owners.

POTTERY

In the cemeteries found at Maiden Castle the dead were buried with a variety of pottery bowls to provide food for their journey to another world. These pots included distinctive shallow bowls known to archaeologists as War-cemetery bowls. Along with most of the other pottery found at Maiden Castle, they were made by a thriving prehistoric pottery industry based in Purbeck and using the ballclays and sands from the tertiary deposits north of the chalk ridge. In fact the distribution of this pottery is one of the ways in which the territory of the Durotriges is defined.

The Durotrigian potters made distinctive bowls, plates, cups, cooking pots and jugs, produced without the aid of a wheel, and finished by burnishing the surface with a bone polisher. The pots were fired in clamps without the use of permanent kilns.

When the Roman army arrived it is clear that the vigorous

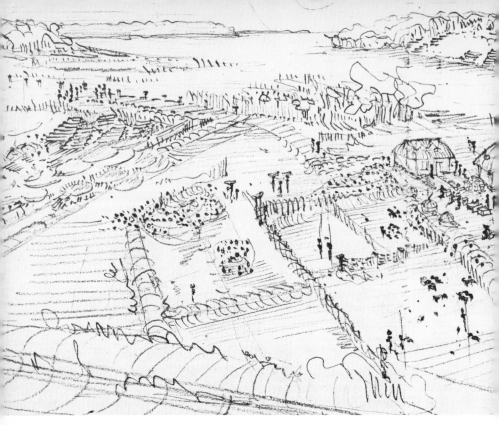

Peter Woodward's drawing of an industrial scene in Purbeck in the Roman period. Various stages of the production of pottery are shown, culminating in the loading of a ship on the right.

pottery industry saw its commercial chance, and there cannot have been much resistance to the invasion in Purbeck.

Within a year or two of its arrival the Second Legion was using Durotrigian pottery of most types in its camps for cooking purposes. It imported samian and other fine wares from Gaul for table use.

As the years passed and the army moved on to the Midlands, Wales, and finally the northern frontiers, the Durotrigian salesmen followed and continued to get the contracts. Other purchases were made of course, but in a typical excavation on Hadrian's Wall, for instance, over 50% of the coarse pottery found will be from the Durotrigian industry. Many boats must have sailed from Poole harbour laden with the products, on their journey to the Tyne at Newcastle and other northern harbours.

At first the traditional Durotrigian shapes were produced. But gradually the potters were influenced by the requirements of their

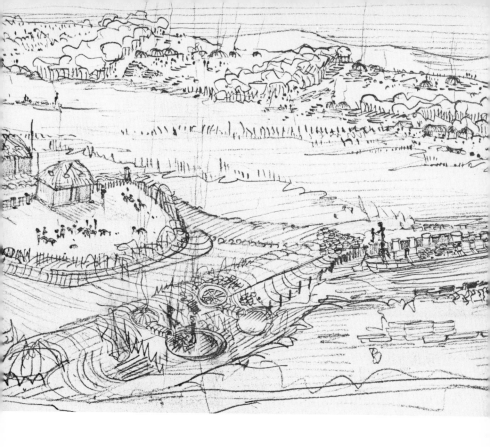

new customers, and new shapes appeared, particularly cooking pots, flange rimmed bowls, and pie dishes.

Amazingly the potters did not change their methods of working. They did not change over to using wheels, and they continued to fire in temporary clamps. Similarly they continued to burnish the pots, with a little token decoration in the form of incised wavy lines. Almost all the pots were intended to be black, and fired with the air excluded in the final stages, to produce that effect.

Not surprisingly this pottery is known to archaeologists as Black Burnished ware. The proof that the pottery on Hadrian's Wall was identical to that found in Dorchester was one of the early triumphs of the scientific approach to archaeology. It was done at Southampton University by the examination of thin sections of pottery under the microscope; this proved that the minerals present in the pots found in the north could only have come from Purbeck.

Black-burnished pottery from Purbeck, the most successful of the industries of the Durotriges. From left to right: a flanged bowl or pie dish, a cooking pot, and a jug. These are all on display in Dorset County Museum.

STONE

The stone found in Roman buildings in Dorset came from a variety of quarries. Dressed stone in the Dewlish villa and coffins from the Poundbury cemetery were made of Hamstone from Ham Hill, near Ilminster. Some Chilmark stone appears at Dewlish also. Portland stone is extensively used for buildings and particularly for fourth century coffins on the island. But the most active industry appears to have been in Purbeck, where a variety of stone types were quarried.

More specialised was Purbeck Marble. This is a shelly limestone which can be cut and polished to a high degree — it has been used in more recent times, and can be seen in the columns of Salisbury cathedral. All the marble appears to have been quarried away in the

A hamstone finial from the roof of the villa at Dewlish.

A newly opened hamstone coffin from the cemetery at Poundbury. The body has been covered in gypsum to preserve it. Details of clothing are preserved on the underside of the gypsum and conditions in such a coffin may enable even hair to survive.

Middle Ages, so it is not clear where the quarries were; but one may have been at Wilkswood, near Langton Matravers. It was moved surprising distances in Roman Britain, and has been found as far away as London and Chester. It was mainly used for finely dressed stone, especially inscriptions. The famous inscription from Chichester mentioning the name of Cogidubnus is of Purbeck marble showing that this industry (which does not seem to have existed before the Romans) had developed early in the history of Roman Britain.

No doubt the Roman taste for marble generated a search in likely areas for a substitute. A temple dedication slab at Verulamium is made of Purbeck marble, as is the tombstone of Carinus at Dorchester.

One unusual industry was based on Kimmeridge shale. This bituminous shale is found at Kimmeridge Bay and had been worked in prehistoric times. It can be burnt as fuel, but more particularly,

A table leg made of Kimmeridge Shale. Many things were made of this material, from bangles to panelling for baths.

An iron window grill from the villa at Hinton St Mary. This is on view at the British Museum along with the famous mosaic floor.

A small industrial furnace found in the excavations on the site of Dorchester hospital.

A black burnished cooking pot let into the floor of a workshop on the Dorchester hospital site. It may have been used for dousing hot iron to temper it.

when newly quarried, can be worked almost like wood, especially on a lathe. It was then polished to a high gloss black finish.

Its uses included the manufacture of bangles, beads, plates, dishes, bowls, and furniture including tables and chairs. There were also decorated trays and architectural features such as wall panels and mosaic tesserae. The cold plunge bath at Dewlish villa was lined with slabs of Kimmeridge shale, and this material too was widely traded across Britain.

OTHER INDUSTRIES

These were the industries which achieved province-wide success. In addition the supply of timber and charcoal was important throughout Dorset, and crystallization of salt from sea water occurred at a number of places along the coast. A whole range of industries were related to farming (for which see chapter 7), including leather working. Cloaks made from British wool were famous as far afield as Rome, and no doubt some came from Dorset.

In the towns there will have been an enormous number of small establishments providing services and products made on the premises, from butchers and greengrocers to metalworkers of every sort. A time traveller to Roman Dorset would find a complex pattern of trade not all that dissimilar to that of the nineteenth and early twentieth century, except that the problems caused by taxation were more akin to the late twentieth century!

X
THE END OF ROMAN RULE

The popular view of the end of Roman Britain is that a sudden decision was taken in Rome to withdraw, and that the legions which arrived in 43 AD packed their bags and marched to the ports, to the cheers of the assembled people. Reality was very much more complex.

For a start, Britain had been under Roman rule for nearly 400 years — the equivalent of the period from Tudor times to the present day. Britain was unquestionably part of the Roman world and shared in its relative prosperity. The departure of Roman armies was something to be feared, as it left the country exposed to attack from outside the frontiers. In Britain's case the threat came from the Picts of Scotland, the Scots of Ireland, and the Saxons and other groups from northern Europe.

The army itself had changed; no longer were the legions the dominant units. Some still existed (the second Augustan was at Richborough) but many were now small infantry regiments. Pride of place was held by cavalry regiments formed to face the attacks of horseborne barbarians from central Europe.

Even the names of civil and military leaders had changed by the fourth century. The military commander on the frontier was known as the Duke of Britain *(Dux Britanniarum)* and the commander responsible for naval defences in the south-east was the Count of the Saxon Shore *(Comes Litoris Saxonici)*. Britain was by now five smaller provinces grouped to form a diocese, and the civilian governor was called the Vicar *(vicarius)*.

A major crisis occurred in 367 AD when the Picts, the Scots and the Saxons apparently conspired (or so the Romans thought) to attack Britain at the same time, and the country was overrun.

It could easily have been the end of Roman Britain. But somehow the central government, itself under severe pressure from barbarian attacks managed to find the resources to rescue Britain. A senior general, Theodosius, spent two years restoring normality, and putting coastal defences and Hadrian's Wall back in working order.

At this time in Dorset we get the first sign of the end. Where

Ackling Dyke passed through the old prehistoric frontier of the tribe's territory at Bokerley Junction, the road was blocked by an extension of the Iron Age dyke. Soon afterwards it was reopened, but we have a glimpse of the civitas of the Durotriges putting their old defences in order to protect themselves from the chaos in other parts of the province. There is not enough evidence to say whether they were successful. There would have been no soldiers in Dorset, but there may have been a town militia to protect Dorchester and Ilchester, and others may have been armed for the occasion in spite of the Roman law which forbade it. Certainly neither towns nor villas show signs of destruction at this date.

Amazingly it is in this very period following the barbarian conspiracy that the towns and villas seem to have reached their greatest prosperity, and this is very difficult to explain, except by an influx of people trying to escape from more troubled areas.

At this time Britain was reasonably well defended. But between 383 and 407 troops were repeatedly withdrawn from Britain to help on the continent, or to intervene on behalf of British commanders who thought they could make a better job of the western emperorship than the man in command at the time. Magnus Maximus took the troops with him in 383, and left chaos behind him. Stilicho restored the situation in 396, only for the adventure to be repeated by Constantine III in 407.

At this point Roman control of Britain lapsed, and it becomes very difficult to know what happened in Britain in any detail. The traditional date for the end of Roman Britain is 410; in that year the civitates of Britain on their own account wrote to the emperor Honorius, explained their plight and what they were doing to help themselves.

Honorius wrote back and told them to see to their own defence. Clearly by this time (probably in 407 or thereabouts) Roman officials had been withdrawn, the vicar's palace in London was empty, and the civil service left without a job. This is proved by the almost complete absence of coins after this date; no one was being paid in Britain by the Roman government, and so no coins came into the country.

In Dorset Bokerley Dyke was closed and opened several times

Bokerley Dyke from the air. This was the pre-Roman frontier of the Durotriges, and was brought back into use after Roman rule from London collapsed in the early fifth century.

around the turn of the century as the Durotriges defended themselves. But this is almost the sum total of archaeological evidence from Dorset, apart from the general decay of the towns, villas and the whole economic structure.

The archaeologist's problem at this period is that coins ceased to be circulated and pottery ceased to be made; at a stroke the two main sources of dating evidence disappear.

At some point in the first decade of the fifth century coins of 402 were dropped in fireplaces built on the mosaics of Dewlish Villa; clearly the buildings were in use, but not in the grand style of its former owners. Nevertheless nothing violent happened. The villa had been cleared of all its possessions and the rooms were empty when weather and decay ultimately led to the collapse of the roof.

Life in Dorchester and Ilchester must have gone on, the walls

The final destruction of Roman Dorchester. Pillars from the verandah of the Roman town house in Colliton Park, Dorchester, deliberately hurled down the well when Durnovaria was in ruins, are removed from the well during the excavations of 1939.

becoming especially significant. Almost certainly a town militia defended them, and a Durotrigian army manned the frontier.

But the whole complex economic structure was collapsing. No money meant a return to the prehistoric practice of barter. Food and shelter were the important things. The markets for pottery and stone products were inaccessible. The industries collapsed and their owners were no longer wealthy. The materials for repairing buildings were not available, and the goods essential to Roman life unobtainable.

The feeling of being shut out of the familiar Roman world must have been depressing indeed.

As the years passed Dorset returned more and more to the pattern of life of its prehistoric past — which had never really disappeared in the countryside anyway. How long the towns survived we cannot yet tell. It must have been well into the fifth century and perhaps even longer.

In the east Saxons and others had been settling for many years already, in some cases by arrangement, in others by force. But they did not reach the south-west in any numbers for another two centuries, and life in Dorset must have gone on.

We have tantalising glimpses of the struggle to keep the Saxons out. We hear of great leaders in Britain heading the resistance; Vortigern, Ambrosius Aurelianus, and Arthur. Victories were won, including a famous one at Mount Badon, which may have been in Dorset.

At South Cadbury in Somerset, and at other sites in the south west, evidence has recently been found of the old hillforts being reoccupied by these sub-Roman leaders. They can be dated, particularly by the wine jars they were importing from the Mediterranean. No such site has been found in Dorset yet, but no major hillfort excavations have taken place in recent years. Mediterranean pottery of the fifth or sixth centuries is said to have been found in Dorchester, but this is uncertain.

In the end Saxon armies and settlers overran Dorset, probably on a large scale in the early seventh century.

After that a new story begins.

PLACES TO VISIT

Maiden Castle. 2 miles south-west of Dorchester on the A354.
Scene of the assault by the second legion.

Hod Hill. 4 miles north-west of Blandford on the A350. Roman fort
inserted into Iron Age hillfort.

South Cadbury Castle. 10 miles north-east of Yeovil on the A303.
Iron Age hillfort re-occupied in the late Roman period by King
Arthur or someone like him.

Badbury Rings. 4 miles north-east of Wimborne. Roman road
junction beside Iron Age hillfort.

Dorchester, Maumbury Rings. Where the Weymouth road crosses
the railway. Roman Amphitheatre.

Dorchester, Carinus tombstone. In St. Georges church,
Fordington, displayed under the tower.

Dorchester, town wall. Surviving fragment just south of the Top o'
Town roundabout.

Dorchester, town house. Displayed behind County Hall.

Dorchester, aqueduct. Follows the Frome valley to the north-west
of Dorchester at least as far as Frampton. Best seen west of
Poundbury hillfort and in Fordington Bottom.

Dorchester, Dorset County Museum. In High West Street; contains
the major collection of archaeological material from the county
including many Roman finds.

Ackling Dyke, Roman road. Join it half a mile south east of
Handley roundabout on the A354 from Blandford to Salisbury
(where the B3081 crosses). The road can be followed from here
south-west towards Badbury Rings for over 9 miles.

Bokerley Dyke, frontier earthwork. The A354 crosses it at
Bokerley Junction, just beyond Woodyates on the way from
Blandford to Salisbury.

Thorncombe Wood, Roman road. 4 miles east of Dorchester near
Higher Bockhampton. The road is visible for over a mile through
Thorncombe Wood into Puddletown Forest.

Villas. No Dorset villa is on view to the public. Finds can be seen
and inquiries made about excavations in progress at the
museums at Dorchester, Poole and Wimborne.

Maiden Castle, Roman temple. The foundations of the temple are
on view in the hillfort — see above.

Jordan Hill, Roman temple. Near Bowleaze Cove, 2 miles east along the coast from Weymouth. Foundations only to be seen.

Industry. None of the industrial sites in Dorset are on display. Finds may be seen in the museums mentioned above.

FURTHER READING

Information about Dorset itself appears mainly in the publications of the Dorset Natural History and Archaeological Society, who can be contacted at Dorset County Museum in High West Street, Dorchester. Their journal, *The Proceedings of the Dorset Natural History and Archaeological Society* has been published annually for over a hundred years. It contains a wealth of information about excavations and discoveries in Dorset. In addition the Society publishes a monograph series in which major excavation reports appear which are too bulky for the *Proceedings*. The Museum will be happy to send an up-to-date list of its publications on receipt of a stamped and addressed envelope.

The second source for Dorset archaeology is the inventory of archaeological monuments produced by the Royal Commission on Historic Monuments; *Dorset* is published in five volumes by HMSO. Dorset is lucky that it has received the attention of the Commission in recent years, and these volumes are the basis of all systematic research in the county.

There are many general books on Roman Britain which provide the background; among the most important are:

Salway. P., *Roman Britain*, (1981)
Frere. S.S., *Britannia*, (1974)
Webster. G., *The Roman Imperial Army*, (1969)
Margary. I.D., *Roman Roads in Britain*, (1974)
Webster. G., *The Roman Invasion of Britain*, (1980)
Wacher. J., *The Towns of Roman Britain*, (1975)
Rivet. A.L.F. ed, *The Roman Villa in Britain*, (1969)
Thomas. A.C., *Christianity in Roman Britain to AD500*, (1981)
Frere. S.S. & St Joseph. J.K.S. *Roman Britain from the Air*, (1983)

JOURNAL: *Britannia*, published annually by the Society for
   Promotion of Roman Studies
MAP: Ordnance Survey, *Map of Roman Britain*, (1978)

Two detailed excavation reports are particularly relevant; these are:

Richmond. I.A.R., *Hod Hill*, (1968)
Wheeler. R.E.M., *Maiden Castle*, (1944)

INDEX